ABANDONED
NEW HAMPSHIRE

ABANDONED
NEW HAMPSHIRE

MICHAEL PETIPAS

AMERICA
THROUGH TIME®
ADDING COLOR TO AMERICAN HISTORY

This book is dedicated to Aisling Petipas, my loving wife, who, through the entirety of this project, showed me nothing but love and support.

I would also like to send my deepest appreciation to Lisa Robinson for recommending me for this project and making this all possible.

America Through Time is an imprint of Fonthill Media LLC
www.through-time.com
office@through-time.com

Published by Arcadia Publishing by arrangement with Fonthill Media LLC
For all general information, please contact Arcadia Publishing:
Telephone: 843-853-2070
Fax: 843-853-0044
E-mail: sales@arcadiapublishing.com
For customer service and orders:
Toll-Free 1-888-313-2665

www.arcadiapublishing.com

First published 2019

ISBN 978-1-63499-137-7

Typeset in Trade Gothic 10pt on 15pt
Printed and bound in England

CONTENTS

ABOUT THE AUTHOR

Michael Petipas was born in Boston, Massachusetts. At age four, his family moved to rural New Hampshire, where he grew up on a 60-acre farm. His life on the farm shaped his love of nature, his adventurous character, and his creative spirit. Mike's love of photography was encouraged by his beloved grandfather, Vincent Petipas (Bubs), who worked as a professional photographer in Boston. Mike continues to find inspiration in the natural beauty of New England and spends many hours hiking in search of the perfect shot. Mike lives in Bristol, New Hampshire, with his wife, Aisling (also an accomplished artist), and dog, Sherman.

INTRODUCTION

I was both excited and nervous to take on this new challenge photographing abandoned buildings throughout New Hampshire. Being primarily a landscape and portrait photographer, this was far outside of my comfort zone. I approach landscape photography by recording what God has already painted. The composition is instinctual, and the rules can be easily applied. In portrait photography, I have to find that there is something unique in every person that I shoot.

Taking photographs of abandoned buildings is one of the most difficult subjects, involving trying to find beauty amongst the wreckage and rubble in places that time forgot. I have to listen to the story that these old and forgotten places are trying to tell. Sometimes the stories are dark and sad, such as the state school in Laconia. In other cases, the buildings were once giants of industry and now slowly lay waste to time and weather. Some places I knew nothing about and would just let my imagination run wild. Some places, such as the Colonial Theatre, I remember fondly from my childhood when the lights from the marque would shine brightly on Main St.

I would lose whole days to bad photo shoots, places I couldn't find, and places I couldn't get into. I would have days where I wasn't sure if I would keep going with the project and then I would have days where I wouldn't trade what I was doing for anything else. Most importantly, I learned from the experience. This project was unique to my previous projects because it added a dose of adrenaline and at times sparked my investigative prowess. It also brought a heightened aspect of imagination into my photographic work, which informed a deeper passion of my love of photography.

It is my hope that this book will be as much as an adventure for you as much as it was for me. I look forward to the next abandoned adventure.

1

COLONIAL THEATRE

Exploring the Colonial Theatre was going to be different from the other places I have explored. I hold a special place in my heart for this relic of my youth. There are a lot of memories inside those walls for me: hanging out with friends, going on first dates, trying to pull the classic yawn and get your arm around a girl, and throwing popcorn at the screen.

Benjamin Piscopo, an Italian immigrant who made his fortune in real estate in Boston, built the Colonial Theatre. Construction began in 1913, and the theatre opened the following year. It was billed as one of the grandest playhouses in all of New England.

It remained a playhouse until around the end of the World War I, when it was converted to a movie theatre. Then, in the 80s, it underwent another conversion and was turned into a multiplex movie cinema. They put up petitions and covered all the ornate paintings, gold leaf, and murals with black curtains and walls.

I remember still being able to see the balconies that sit stage right and stage left if you happened to see a movie in the far right or far left movie theatre. The main stage was converted to another theatre. This can be seen in the picture of the door with the number 5 on the wall. The seating was still in place on the stage for the most part, along with parts of the old movie screen that sat to the side of the stage.

Then, in 2001, after eighty-seven years, the Colonial Theatre closed its doors and has remained closed since. There is currently an effort through the Belknap EDC, Town of Laconia, and 603 Main Street, to bring the old playhouse back to life through donations. A few years back, they raised enough money to begin gutting the multiplex, but then ran out of funds—they are currently trying to raise enough money to keep going with the restoration.

As I entered through the same double doors I would have entered through so many years ago, it was exactly as I remembered: the ticket booth to my right, the red wallpaper on the walls, the uphill walk to yet another set of double doors, where the old ticket checker would stand tearing stubs. Beyond that was the snack concessions off to the right as you walked in, and to the left stood a massive grandfather clock that is no longer there. From there you would get your popcorn, milk duds, and a coke and walk through yet another set of double doors and head to the theatre and wait for your movie to start. The hallways were just like the lobby—they had also been left the way I remember, with blue reflective wallpaper and sconce lighting.

From this point on, what I photographed was not what I remembered as a kid. What I saw was what was under those dividers and curtains. I saw what this place looked like in its glory. It was unbelievably preserved: the ornate gold leaf everywhere, the murals, and the columns. The stage sat looming in the dark, larger than life. I imagined those old cranky muppets sitting in the booths of to the side of the stage. I imagined the band warming up in the orchestra pit, and the low muffled voices of people slowly filing in.

This old theatre is a special place for countless people that have many memories here. It is my hope that the Belknap EDC, 603 Main St, and the City of Laconia succeed in bringing the old Colonial Theatre back to life.

Right: The main entrance to the Colonial Theatre located on Main St. Laconia, NH.

Below: The original stage of the Colonial Theatre. The artwork and gold leaf is unbelievably preserved for its age, most likely due to being covered up during the many renovations that took place over the years.

Standing up in the right balcony, looking down at the stage, main floor, and left balcony.

The stage was converted into movie theatre #5. Most of the seats are still there and you can see the entrance to the cinema on stage left.

The main floor of the theatre from the left side.

Looking at the stage from under the second-floor balcony seating. The date 1914 above the stage signifies the year that the theatre was completed.

Looking down the first-floor hallway towards one of two entrances to the main floor of the theatre.

Looking down the hallway back towards the double doors that would lead to the lobby and snack concessions.

Above: Second-floor balcony looking down on main stage.

Right: Center of second-floor balcony looking down at the main stage.

Second-floor balcony looking at main stage.

What remains of seating on the right side of the second-floor balcony.

Looking down the second-floor hallway from the far left.

Looking down at the stage from the second-floor balcony

Looking towards the double doors that lead to Main St. from the lobby. The original ticket booth can be seen on the left of the picture.

The original ticket booth to the theatre that was still used when the Colonial was a Cineplex.

Looking out at Main St., Laconia from the main lobby. This has always been the main entrance to the theatre.

Looking towards the double doors that would lead to the concession stand. The ticket booth is to the left and the main entrance is just behind me.

The projection room from when the Colonial was a movie Cineplex. Some of the old reels and movie projector are still there.

Looking at the crown of the main stage.

Above: Looking at one of the many hand painted murals above the main stage.

Right: The entrance to movie theatre #5.

Left: The remains of seating that was in movie theatre #5. This would have been located on the main stage.

Below: Seating for movie theatre #5 that was located on the main stage.

Even though the Colonial Theatre has been closed for years they still light up the Marque on Main St. in Laconia.

2

FORT STARK

Fort Stark is located on Jerry's Point on the southeastern tip of New Castle Island in New Hampshire. This was by far the oldest site that I visited with a history that dates to 1746, when the fort was first fortified and named Fort Cumberland at the time. It was rebuilt in 1775 for the American Revolution, but the guns (two thirty-two pounders and six twenty-four pounders) were removed to arm other forts in the surrounding area. The fort was rearmed in 1775 and garrisoned until 1778.

Most of what you are looking at when you are there is not from this time period, but rather a mix of existing structures that date back to Spanish American War and continue through the years to World War II, when Battery Kirk was built in the middle of the fort and disguised to look like a seaside mansion to provide cover for its true nature as a radar station.

After the war in 1948, the fort was decommissioned and turned over to the Navy in 1950. The Navy used the fort as harbor defense until 1953 After that, it became a training center for the Navy's Mobile Inshore Undersea Warfare Unit until 1980. Fort Stark is now owned by the State of New Hampshire and is open for the public to walk the grounds; however, the inside of the fort is closed off, with fencing and barbed wire.

I visited Fort Stark on a cold November afternoon. I loaded up my dog, Sherman, and my wife into the truck and headed south towards the coast. The foliage had long since dropped and we had experienced a couple of snowstorms already, but nothing that would stick for very long. I love the coast this time of year. There aren't a lot of people around, and there is something refreshing about the cold air blowing off the ocean. The skies were blue this day, and there were just enough clouds to make for interesting long exposures.

I pulled in to the small parking lot at the end of the road and let my dog out, who immediately ran past the gate and onto the old parade ground. My wife went after him and I began to get my camera equipment ready on the tailgate of my truck while going through my mental checklist: check the batteries and flash settings and clean off the lenses. I shouldered my backpack and took off to take some exterior shots and find my wife and dog, and hopefully find a way into this fort.

I decided I was going to have to climb the fence in order to get the shots I really wanted. I took off my camera backpack and instructed my wife to throw it over the fence to me after I was on the other side. Once on the other side, I headed down a steep set of stairs and headed towards what remained of the main gun battery.

I found a large rusty steel door that was ajar, and was able to squeeze through into the dark interior. I was certainly not the first one to be in here. There was graffiti all over the walls and empty beer cans scattered randomly. At first, I thought this was going to be one or maybe two small rooms, but it was a whole network of rooms and hallways that weaved under the entire fort. My heart started to beat faster; this was exciting, this is when it pays off, and this is when you get involved in the unexpected. There was room after room with this shower-style tile that had started to crumble off the walls. I am guessing that these rooms were ammo storage, judging by the rail system that was still suspended from the ceiling, but I'm not sure. There were other rooms and hallways that led to large exterior steel doors that had been welded shut from the outside.

When I finally emerged, the sun had started to go down. I was happy how the day had gone. I found my wife and dog playing an intense game of fetch down by the water and decided to join in before heading home.

Looking at the backside of the radar building at Fort Stark. This building was designed to look like a seaside mansion of the day to allude the enemy during the start of WWII.

Looking towards the right side of the radar station.

This was an unknown small outbuilding to the rear of the fort. It sits just above the old dock pylons.

The front of the radar building that would look out the east and open ocean.

Underneath Fort Stark there was a network of various rooms and hallways, all containing the rail system, visible on the ceiling, for what I assume would have been moving ammo for the main battery.

The main hallway beneath Fort Stark that had what appeared to be storage rooms all along the left side of the corridor. Here you can also see the rail system that was most likely used for moving the large shells for the cannons that were mounted above.

This was one of the storage rooms that was off the main hallway under the fort; however, unlike the other rooms, this does not have the rail system on the ceiling.

This is currently the administration building at Fort Stark.

This is another room that I believe was used for storage underneath the fort.

Standing at the back of one of the storage rooms, looking back towards were the hallway.

One of what I believe to be the ammo storage rooms. Here you can see the rail system on the ceiling.

This is the end of the hallway. The door at the rear exits to the outside of the fort towards the backside of the compound.

The main hallway under Fort Stark. This picture does a good job of showing how the rail system would exit a storage room and proceed on these rails to an elevator that would then lift the shells for the cannons to the topside.

Looking at an open door into one of the rooms from the main hallway under the fort.

Exterior picture of small outbuilding at Fort Stark

Looking at one of the many locked doors that lead underneath the fort. I did not gain access through one of these doors, because they are all welded shut.

There was one door that I was able to squeeze through along the side of the fort that led to more rooms. I am not sure what they were used for.

Another picture of the radar station designed to look like a seaside mansion of the day.

This is the first building next to the administration building that you see as you walk onto the old parade grounds of Fort Stark.

3

KIMBALL CASTLE

Kimball Castle, located in Gilford, NH, is the former summer estate of Benjamin Ames Kimball. The old castle sits on the top of Lockes Hill, overlooking Lake Winnipesaukee and the surrounding Belknap and White Mountains. The castle was originally built in 1894 by Italian stonemasons using locally sourced materials, and it is situated on what was once a 300-acre estate. The estate has long since been subdivided, with the exception of 20 acres where the castle sits.

After Benjamin Ames Kimball's death in 1920, the castle stayed in the family until 1960, when Charlotte Kimball, the last heir to the property, died. After that, the castle began to fall into a state of disrepair. Then, in 1981, the town of Gilford took over the property and the castle was added to the National Registry of Historical Places, but remained abandoned.

This is an impressive structure with unbelievable craftsmanship that is evident both from the exterior and interior. Made of cut granite and fashioned in a medieval style, the three-and-a-half-story castle dominates the skyline as you approach from the trail. The trail is what once was the original driveway and two giant stone columns greet you as you walk up to the top of Lockes Hill.

The interior is in relatively good shape considering the age of the structure. Most of the old oak paneling is still intact, along with the oak columns and banisters. This is mostly because the old slate roof never gave way. The winters here in New England don't lend themselves well to abandoned properties. Once the roof goes, you only have a couple years before the snow load collapses the structures, and in some cases renders nothing more than a pile of old rotten lumber.

It would be nice to one day see this old castle restored to its former glory, but for now, it remains atop Lockes Hill through the heat of summer and cold of winter, slowly becoming less and less of the grand residence that it once was.

The second floor of Kimball Castle has a skylight that looks down on the main hall below. The roof and skylight are watertight, and this has played a major role in the maintenance of the interior woodwork.

Looking at the second-floor bedroom entrances from the top of the stairs.

Above: Another look at the second floor from the top of the stairs. It is rumored that the woodwork was completed in England and then shipped to NH to be reassembled.

Left: The second floor of Kimball Castle.

Right: The main hall of Kimball Castle shot from a small alcove. One of two kitchen doors is off to my left. The other kitchen door is on the other side of the fireplace not visible in this picture.

Below: The door to the far left is one of two entrances to the kitchen. This entrance cuts through what I believe to be the remains of the pantry. The second door leads to a small bathroom.

Looking towards the kitchen from the main hall.

The main hall shot from the entrance to the castle.

The main hall with the door to the porch that overlooks the lake to the left.

The main hall looking towards the outside deck and the main set of stairs to the second floor. The second set of stairs takes off from the kitchen.

This is one of the three entrances to the castle. There are two doors on the front of the building. The third entrance is on the right side, off the building under an awning.

An exterior shot of the upper windows of the castle. Italian stonemasons were imported to build the castle and their craftsmanship really shows around the widows, door jams, and along the roofline.

Exterior picture of the castle showing the entirety of the structure. Lake Winnipesaukee would have been visible from three sides of the castle back in the day. Today, because of overgrowth, you can only see it from the porch on the backside of the castle.

The porch on the back side of Kimball Castle has large granite arches and impeccable views of Lake Winnipesaukee from all sides.

4

LACONIA STATE SCHOOL

Laconia State School was founded on the idea that feeble mindedness (a common phrase in the 1900s for people with developmental disabilities) was not just a shortcoming, but a moral flaw. It was decided that a facility would be built in Laconia, NH, and in 1903, the New Hampshire School for the Feeble Minded opened.

It wasn't until 1924 that the school went through a name change to the Laconia State School, but it already had a reputation as a horrid and inhumane place to end up. By 1916, overcrowding had become a serious problem and the eugenic movement of the time made it an acceptable practice to sterilize these poor people under the belief that the feeble mindedness was a genetic flaw that could be passed down to offspring.

Overcrowding became even more of a problem during the Great Depression, when families that were struggling would send their children there so that they would at the very least get a hot meal. There were requests to the NH legislature for years, but the requests were ignored, and by 1942, there were over 600 residents with many people being forced to sleep on the floors of the barren facilities due to even more overcrowding.

This overcrowding and minimal care for the residents of the Laconia State School continued into the 70s when a court order required a population reduction of the people living there. It was decided shortly after that the state of NH would just slowly reduce residents until there were none left. This was accomplished in 1991 when the Laconia State School closed its doors.

After the state school closed, part of the 240-acre grounds were converted into a prison, and this remained in service until 2009. This was only a small portion of the place, and most of the original outbuildings were not incorporated into the prison.

This is a dark and haunting place with a terrible past that many would like to forget. It was a dark chapter for the state of New Hampshire for the inhumane treatment of the developmentally disabled.

The Spaudling building is one of the many structures that sit on the grounds of the old Laconia State School. I do not know what this building was used for.

The Baker building is one of four buildings on what was known as the quad. These buildings were used as dormitories for the residents of the Laconia State School.

Looking through the fence and razor wire at the prison on the grounds of the school.

Looking north towards what was known as the quad. The quad consisted of the Baker building along with Felker, Blood, and Keyes. These buildings were used as dormitories.

I believe this is the Keys building, one of the dormitories used at the school.

Looking at what I believe is the Keys building from another angle.

Another one of the many buildings on the grounds of the Laconia State School. You can see the prison complex off to the left.

Another look at the Keys building.

5

L. W. PACKARD MILL

The L. W. Packard Mill is an old textile mill in the middle of downtown Ashland, NH, that had been in operation from the 1840s all the way up until the 90s, when it closed its doors for good. At one time, the mill was a centerpiece for the small town of Ashland, employing over 300 people.

I spoke with a local kid that was hanging outside a convenience store on the corner. He warned me not to go in there. He told me, "That's is where the junkies go to shoot up." Great, I thought to myself, and headed down what used to be the drive to the main parking lot of the plant.

I was walking around the exterior of the old textile mill, taking some shots. I noticed a truck parked across the way watching me. I pretended not to see the truck and kept shooting in hopes to get as much material as I could before the inevitable, "Hey, this is private property." The truck door opened and a couple in their mid-thirties stepped out and crossed the main road towards me. They walked up and we exchanged pleasantries. Fortunately, they were just curious as to what I was doing. As it would turn out, these two were planning on opening a liquor distillery in part of the old mill and had a key to the main building. This was fantastic, as it would have been next to impossible to get into this part of the mill. We entered the old mill and began to walk from floor to floor. They were more than happy to exchange what historical information they knew about the old mill, and told me about their plans for the distillery that they were going to build in the future. We slowly worked our way up to the top floor of the factory, where there were large recessed windows that surrounded the room. I was told that this was where the women that would sew garments during the turn of the century would sit to utilize as much daylight as possible to do the meticulous stitching work. The hardwood floors were still in decent shape and the bleach pine boards on the walls were for the most part in close to original condition. There were still measurements written in pencil on the walls of each sewing station by the windows. This part of the mill had been nothing but empty space for a long time. Even when the mill was in full operation, the upstairs floor wasn't used for much, except maybe storage.

We continued back down to the ground level. The couple that had let me into the building said they could unlock the door to the basement if I wanted to take a look, but they would go no further. They also knew about the junkies that would frequent this space and thought it too dangerous.

I walked through the door and down four or five steps into darkness. I turned on my head lamp, but the space was too vast for the beam to illuminate all the way to the back of the room. This is when your head starts to play games. This is when you must calm yourself and remember why you are there. You have to forget that there could be a bunch of lunatics hiding in the shadows, just beyond the reach of your light. I could hear the river rushing underneath the floor. I could see giant holes in floor that if you fell through you would end up in the river below. I was starting to become irrational. I started to imagine junkies without pigment from lack of sun coming out of the shadows and tossing me in one of those holes. The last thing I would ever hear would be, "YOU DON'T BELONG HERE." I knew that as soon as the flash on my camera was triggered, if there were other people in the building with me, they were going to know I was there, if they didn't already know. I felt like someone could see me, but I couldn't see them.

I took a deep breath and began to shoot. The camera flash exploded into the darkness. My heart was racing, and I had to steady my hand. I had to make sure my settings were correct. I had to make sure I made it back alive so that I could write this.

Looking up the side of the main building towards the old stack.

This is a photograph of one of the many buildings that are on the grounds of the L. W. Packard Mill.

Looking at the front of one of the many buildings in the vast L. W. Packard complex.

Looking across the bridge from Main St. at the L. W. Packard Mill buildings. The bridge crosses the river that runs beneath the main building, supplying power to the mill through hydro turbines. These turbines are online despite the mill being closed and are looked after by a single power plant operator.

The first floor of the L. W. Packard Mill. From the 1840s up until the early 90s, this vast empty space would have been busting with activity and a cacophony of noise from the many looms and other equipment.

An old doorway on the second floor of the L. W. Packard Mill. I'm unsure what this would have led to originally. Now, it opens to empty space that looks down onto the first floor.

Second floor of the mill. You can see the old doorway that opens to empty space and looks down to the first floor towards the rear of the photo on the right.

Above: Measurements most likely written down by the seamstresses that worked at these window stations.

Right: There was an unexplained single red tree painted next to one of the old sewing stations. It doesn't seem like it was graffiti, as all the other walls were untouched.

One of the many recessed windows that surround the room that were originally sewing stations.

This is the third floor of the L. W. Packard Mill, photographed from roughly the middle of the room and towards the left side. This room was well preserved and had seen no vandalism. It felt as if someone locked it years ago and nobody had been up there since.

The rooftop of the third floor. This was just outside of where the recessed windows of the sewing stations were. It shows the size of the L. W. Packard Mill.

This is another shot of the third floor from the rear and to the right of the room.

This was the first room you enter in the basement. The stairs up to the first floor were just to my left. The basement was divided into two rectangular rooms, with the second room being the largest.

This is the second room in the basement of the L. W. Packard Mill.

This is another photograph of the second room of the L. W. Packard Mill. The hole in the floor in the foreground of the picture drops straight down to the river that is rushing below the factory. This was an unsettling sight, as it looked as though the floor had collapsed. I couldn't help but wonder how secure the space was.

Another photograph of the second floor.

I assume that this was an office or perhaps an old control room to the power plant. The windows to the left of the picture look into the rooms in the basement and the widows to the right look out at the river that is running directly below you.

Exterior of the buildings of the L. W. Packard Mill. The buildings in the far back are part of the same complex.

6

REDSTONE QUARRY

In the heart of North Conway, New Hampshire, lies the unincorporated town of Redstone, home of the long-time abandoned Redstone Quarry. It began operation in 1886 by the North Jay Granite Company of Maine. By 1888, Redstone was in full operation, with the small town of Redstone built around the mine. The small village was complete with a school, church, railroad station, dance hall, company store, and housing for employees.

Redstone got its name from the red and pink color that is found in the granite that was mined from this area. At one time, it was one of the largest granite quarries in New England and no doubt contributed to the state of New Hampshire's nickname, the "granite state." There are many local bridges and buildings, and in the local cemetery you can see the massive slabs of granite that had been mined from the side of Rattlesnake Mountain. One of these buildings is the old train station in downtown Laconia, NH, that I had a chance to check out while I was in the area shooting the Colonial Theatre.

I left later than I would have liked this particular afternoon and wasn't really sure how to find the old quarry. All I knew was that it was going to be around the base of Rattlesnake Mountain. I ended up parking behind the Wal-Mart on East West Road in North Conway and decided to start walking up the power lines towards the base of Rattlesnake. I knew I was in the right vicinity—what I didn't know was what I was going to find up there: old cellar holes or piles of rubble that just didn't lend itself to anything of interest, maybe I wouldn't find anything at all.

I hiked to where there was a single tract trail that broke from the power lines and headed uphill towards the base of Rattlesnake Mountain. I decided to give this a try, as it felt like it was headed in the right direction. I climbed uphill about a half mile and as I rounded a sharp corner, there stood an old building just sitting there in the middle of the woods. This would appear to be the old barracks for the workers. I thought this was certainly a good start.

From here, the trail broke in four different directions, and once again I had to decide what direction I should take. I decided to continue uphill towards the base of the mountain. I only had to hike a couple hundred yards, and there in the overgrown brush sat the old giant lathes that were used for turning and polishing the massive granite blocks.

I have seen lathes before, both for turning metal and wood, but never have I seen anything on this large of a scale. What remained of a polishing lathe sat in a crumbling tin building and another turning lathe was sitting out in the open. Off to my left was what looked like the remains of a highline system that came down from the quarry.

From here, it was evident what direction to take, as the trail was lined with old granite tailings and what remained of an old mining cart track. I followed the old tracks up another short hike to where they were clearly cutting the granite from the face of the mountain. There was an old highline still standing in front of the flat-cut granite wall with a massive bull wheel sitting at its base. There was another tin structure that had fully collapsed, but you could still see the old motors and pulleys buried beneath the tin.

After spending some time exploring and taking pictures, I decided to venture on, although the direction I should take became unclear once again. I decided to follow a little single-track trail that followed along the base of the mountain and see what else I could find. I walked a ways on a pretty level terrain until I came upon a massive pile of granite tailings. It looked like a granite waterfall that started all the way at the top of Rattlesnake Mountain and ended far below me. These were beautiful pieces of stone that were discarded for various reasons. Some looked like nothing more than rocks you would find in your backyard, while some of the other pieces had been cut into massive tables, post, and pillars with the feather and wedge marks running along the outside edges of the massive granite slabs.

Redstone Quarry remained in operation until around 1948 when lower demand for cut granite due to cheaper building materials forced them out of business. All that remains of this once thriving town today is a few outbuildings, some old machinery, and the occasional old timer around town that remembers it from back in the day.

Turnbuckle in the ceiling of the old bunkhouse at Redstone.

Second floor of the bunkhouse at Redstone.

Left: What appears to be old mailboxes located at the base of the stairs in the old bunkhouse.

Below: The remains of an old highline system found by the granite lathes. Most likely this was used to ferry granite slabs down the hill to the large granite lathes.

Above: One of two lathes used in turning and polishing granite mined from the base of Rattlesnake Mountain.

Right: The remains of a structure containing one of the two lathes that are still on site at Redstone.

Looking down the lathe that is still in the remains of the buildings found uphill of the bunkhouse.

A manufacturers tag on one of the lathes.

Looking at the other end of the lathe that is located inside the remains of the old outbuilding.

Manufacturers label on the lathe that sits outside. It reads: FR Patch MFG CO. Rutland, VT.

The main quarry located at the base of Rattlesnake Mountain.

This is what I assume is the remains of the top end of the highline system that was used to ferry granite down to the lathes located a couple hundred yards below.

This was a collapsed outbuilding up by the main quarry and contained the remains of old engines and some sort of pulley system; however, I am not sure what it would have been used for.

Another look at the remains of what I believe to be the other end of a highline system that was in place to ferry granite.

A large pile of granite tailings that are located a couple hundred yards away from the main quarry along the base of the mountain.

A look at both lathes in the background; I am unsure what this piece of machinery is in the foreground.

7

RUSTY OLD BUICK

Alexandria, New Hampshire, is a small town in Grafton County, NH, that sits at the base of Mt. Cardigan. Alexandria is one of those off-the-map towns in NH—unless you got lost on back roads and stumbled across it, you would never know that it was there. Incorporated in the late 1700s, it consist of nothing more than a church, town hall, and small one-room library in the center of town.

If you ever want to feel like you have gone back in time, this is the sort of town that you would want to visit. It looks like one of those Budweiser post cards that you see around Christmas time, with the snow covered church steeple and wagon being pulled through the snow by a team of horses. It's how I wished all the small towns around me had remained, before the gas stations and the dreaded dollar stores that plague small town America with their cheap disposable garbage for sale popped up.

There are no major roads leading in or out of this classic New England colonial town. I would have to stick to the back roads to get there. This was exactly what I was doing without knowing where I was going exactly. I had just started driving that morning with real no plan or destination. I turned onto some random back road coming out of Bristol, NH.

The pavement soon gave way to dirt and the houses started to become few and far between. *What a place to live in the winter,* I thought to myself as my truck barreled over the washboard roads. I wondered how long it took for the plow to reach them. I bet many had fallen in love with living out this far in the summer, and quickly fell out of love in the winter, when the realities of being trapped in the middle of nowhere set in.

Heavily forested roads would break way to old farms that dotted the landscape, places that were built at the turn of the century and were probably passed down through the generations.

I was starting to lose hope that I would come across anything but trees and dirt as I dropped down into the valley of Mt Cardigan. I was driving along a small brook when a collapsed house appeared hidden back with the tall pines.

I parked in a pull off across the street that was most likely for people to park and fish the river. I let my dog out and grabbed my camera. This place had been left to rot in the woods for some time. The snow had collapsed the roof of the main house that was half singlewide trailer that someone had put an addition on. The old wrap-around deck was rotten and half laying on the ground. There was an old camper that was heavily overgrown. An old Buick sat there in pretty good shape. I wondered how long the car had been there and why nobody had taken it.

My best guess is nobody except for the locals knows that it's hidden back in the woods. The family that owned it has long since left and most likely this was just a summer home. Even still, here it sits unmolested and left alone. There are no signs of the spray-paint, broken windows, or signs of vandalism that are prevalent in more densely populated areas. The only vandal there was time and the snow.

Above: The house that was found in Alexandria, NH, along with an old camper and old car.

Right: An old outhouse located on the Alexandria property.

A look from the kitchen back towards the bedroom of the old camper.

A look at the kitchen counter in the camper in Alexandria.

The bedroom of the old camper.

Side view of the old car in Alexandria.

Front view of the old car in Alexandria.

The remains of the camper in Alexandria.

Looking at the layout of the property with the main house and old car.

A bedroom from the main house. This was the only shot I was able to get from the interior of the main house. I took this through an open window.

8

STRATTON AND CO. FLOUR MILL

Stratton and Co. Flour Mill is located on the banks of the Merrimack River in Boscawen, New Hampshire. This area of New Hampshire was a giant of industry at the turn of the century, with mills that were in operation up and down the mighty Merrimack River using its water for power and producing all manner of goods. Examples include the Dustin Island Woolen Mill, J. E. Seymonds Table Co. Factory, Ralfs Sash and Door Manufacturing, Contocook Mill, Penacook Mill, and Concord Axle Works. It is here that you will find the Stratton and Co. Mill.

It was pouring rain on the day that I decided to visit the abandoned Flour Mill. I was hoping that the rain would add some nice affect to the photo's as it cascaded through the holes in the roof of the rotting mill. The rain is definitely my least favorite weather to take pictures in. I have done it before, but don't like it. It's almost impossible to keep your lenses clear and gear dry. In the past, I have ruined whole photo shoots from a wet smear on the lens I never noticed.

I parked in a pull out by the railroad tracks down the road so that I would not draw attention to myself. I put on a light rain jacket and walked towards the old mill. I snuck in through a hole in the bricks at the east side of the building. I was inside a lower floor with the now flooded Merrimack River rushing below me. The rain was lightly pattering on the old rotting floor as it leaked down from the top floors. There were old windows and holes in the wall on the riverside of the building that was adding this spattering of light over the otherwise dimly lit space. I wondered if I would be able to get any further than this first floor as I took my camera gear out of my backpack.

I started to snap pictures as I walked towards the west side of the old flour mill. Through an open window, I could see that the Merrimack River had breached its banks from the heavy rains and was up along the edge of the brick. The water rushed with whitecaps, around the trees that would normally be sitting on dry land, and made the banks of the river look like an infinity pool that you would not want to take a swim in.

I found a rotten set of stairs towards the backside of the mill that would take me to the upper floors. I had to decide how much I was willing to risk getting the pictures I was looking for. If I walked away, I would have to scrap the whole thing. I just didn't have enough material out of that bottom floor to consider using any of it for the book. My heart was racing, and I realized for the first time that no one knew where I was. I put my left hand on the old rusty railing and my right foot on the first runner of the stairs, mustered my courage, and started up the rotten stairs.

I was now standing on the second floor and looking out the windows at the flooded Merrimack rushing well over the banks below me. I took a minute to consider that the flooded river could wash this whole place away with me in it. I then quickly dismissed that thought as quickly as it had popped into my head and decided to carry on.

I continued picking my way across the rotten floors and then up rotten stairs until I had made it to the fourth floor of the Stratton Flour Mill. I stood on the top of the mill and took a deep breath. I had made it, and to be honest I felt this odd sense of pride in getting as far as I had. This was quickly extinguished by the realization that I had to now go back the way I came. I had to make my way back down those dreaded four floors. It reminded me of when I was a kid, climbing trees for fun. I was always so focused on getting to the top that I would often not think about getting down.

I picked my way back to the bottom floor and stepped out into the rain. I remember just wanting a drink of water and how happy I was to be standing in the rain that I had hated hours before.

Underneath the Stratton Mill. The stairs to the upper floors are located at the far end, out of view in this picture.

This is the far end of the bottom floor of the Stratton Mill. The stairs to the upper floors are located next to the open door in the right of the picture.

This is an adjacent building that I was unable to enter do to the seriousness of decay. I took this photograph from the third floor of the main building.

This is the second floor of the Stratton Mill, looking out at the swollen Merrimack River.

Above: A pair of tanks on the third floor of the mill.

Left: The tanks located on the third floor of the mill.

Above left: Looking out the window of the second floor with the Merrimack River in the background.

Above right: Another look at the second floor.

Left: Looking at the third floor of the mill.

Below: Bottom floor of the Stratton Mill. This was where I entered the building.

The exterior of the Stratton and Co. Mill.

The bottom floor of the Stratton Mill.

9

TRAIN CAR 3209

In Bartlett, a small town in the heart of the White Mountain National Forest, you can find abandoned train cars sitting of to the side of the main track for the Conway Scenic Railroad. I had heard about this spot from a friend of mine who had found these abandoned train cars while skiing up in that area the winter before.

It was the first weeks of October when I decided I would give finding these trains a try. I had been working up in Tamworth that night, so I decided it only made sense that I leave from there in the morning. I decided to take the Kancamagus Highway out of Conway, and then cut down to the center of Bartlett via Bear Notch Road.

It was peak foliage and the mountains around me were exploding with color. I quickly got a second wind as the sun began to illuminate the gold, orange, and red trees that covered the mountainsides. This was one of the better foliage years, with everything turning at the same time, making for a landscape that was almost surreal. Driving through the National Forest this time of year is like driving through a dream. It was quiet this early in the morning and I felt like I had the whole of the White Mountains to myself. The leaf peepers had yet to wake up or finish breakfast and start swarming all over the two-lane roads. I had those hills to myself and it felt good to run down that mountain into Bartlett, with the window open letting the cold morning air into the cab of the truck, with a fresh cup of coffee working its magic on my sleepless night.

I pulled into the center of Bartlett and crossed the railroad tracks. I looked left and right, but there was no train. I started to drive up side streets that followed the tracks, looking for the old train. It didn't appear to be to the north, so I turned the truck around and started to investigate to the south. I pulled into the Bartlett Elementary School and decided to take a look down the tracks. There it was—black against the burning colors of fall, just sitting there like it was still waiting for passengers to board. I almost couldn't believe it. The story from my friend just seemed too good to be true. I grabbed my camera gear and headed down the tracks towards the old passenger cars in the woods. I was taking pictures as I went, keeping an eye out for other trains that might be coming down the still active track.

I can't help but wish that train travel is still prevalent in America the way it used to be. It must have been nice to live in a city like Boston and hop on a train to head north for the weekend, watching the mountains, fields, and rivers fly by from the window. It must have been a spectacular journey this time of year, with the trees all around exploding with color.

I boarded the old train from the rear and began to make my way forward through the train cars, taking pictures as I went. I was tired, but I was having a lot of fun. These train cars were in great shape and the golden light of fall shining through the windows of the train had a calming effect. It was quiet and peaceful in there.

I finished taking pictures and decided to hang out and soak in the colors and beauty of the mountains this time of year.

The old train sits on tracks to nowhere, as though it's going to get hooked up an hauled away to some unknown destination.

Photographed from the other side looking towards the town of Bartlett, NH, and where Bear Notch Rd. crosses the tracks.

The entrance to the train located between the first and second passenger cars.

I walked along the train to the third passenger car at the rear. This is the place I entered. Other than the graffiti that was all over the walls and ceilings, this train car was in relatively good shape.

Here is another shot of the first train car looking back towards the second car.

The second train car wasn't in nearly the same shape of the first car. I assume the seats were pulled by the railroad to be repurposed in one way or another.

The doors that separate the first and second passenger car.

This is a photograph of the third and last passenger car on the train. It was in better shape than the second car, but not as good as the first.

Seats from the third passenger car.

The door that exits the second passenger car and enters the third passenger car.

Above: The side doors to the passenger cars.

Right: A photograph of the coupling used to hold train cars together.

This was on one of the passenger cars and the only number that was still visible.

The train, looking towards North Conway from Bartlett, NH.